Smoke and Mirrors

Smoke and Mirrors: Making the Transformation to Nonsmoker a Path of Spiritual and Personal Growth.

A Handbook.

Hidden Owl Books
www.hiddenowlbooks.com

Front cover painting, "Two Women," by Sharon Levine.
Design and layout by Richard Levine.
Grateful acknowledgment to Novel Development Corp. for the woodcuts.

www.TheDoubleMessage.com

For bulk orders or special editions for your organization, visit one of the websites list on this page, or write to Richie@rocketmail.com

Dedicated to Warren Goldberg, who taught me when not to eat a bagel.

CONTENTS

HOW TO USE THIS BOOK

You can read it, or not read it, however you wish. Although its consistency would probably make less than ideal cigarette paper, it might serve as a good dart target or close-quarter fly swatter. It is designed, however, to be read slowly, with liberal use of the lined pages to record your thoughts. (If this is a library copy, please use your own notebook.) Once used, it will be as uniquely yours as the matrix of your personal smoking history, and your reasons for smoking.

The sections are not numbered. It is your journey, your path, your itinerary. Number them if you like. The chef prepares the dish, he doesn't come out and supervise the chewing. Chew over this material in whatever manner and order makes sense to you. It asks questions. You supply the answers. Add your own questions. Give yourself space to digest them.

The first half invites you to explore possibly heretofore hidden aspects of your relationship with tobacco. The second half facilitates your commitment. The first person references are Cynthia's; her journal excerpts in the appendix are included as example, not blueprint. Your writing ought to be as individually yours as you surely are.

Presumingly, you are a smoker. Nevertheless, this book neither attempts to persuade you to quit, nor takes any position on any particular techniques. It's about self-clarity and empowerment.

INTRODUCTION

Smoke and Mirrors describes the book's essence: delusion and truth hidden behind a veil of smoke. Like seers using mirrors in a dark smoky room, the habit of smoking also contains delusion. A smoker might think she is doing one thing, such as just having a relaxing cigarette break, when in truth she is avoiding a feeling or task. The process of discovering and driving out is a definition of smoking: like smoking a woodchuck from his hole.

Examining your smoking habit can ferret out how, when, and where you delude yourself. Mirrors can trick. But mirrors can also reveal. This book invites you to discover who you are by looking in this mirror, to learn by seeing yourself through the reflection of your habit.

Smoking is a ritual. Native American ceremonies and the Catholic Mass use smoke to connect matter and spirit. Other examples of ritual are sitting on a barstool, musing on the front porch, and watching a movie with your significant other.

The commitment called for to quit smoking can elicit spiritual and personal growth. But it is a individual process. What is helpful for one person may not be helpful for another. Courageous self-examination can evoke the spiritual connection to secure your status as a nonsmoker.

THE DOUBLE MESSAGE

Imagine sitting in a comfortable chair below a large "**NO SMOKING**" sign next to a blackened lung antismoking poster. On the coffee table rests an ash tray, elegant lighter, and pack of your favorite brand.

Recognize the double message? Do you stress yourself thinking, "I should give up smoking," then

convince yourself you deserve this pleasure? Do
well-meaning friends and family
explain why you must quit,
showing you yet anther article
on its detrimental effects, as if
they think you have forgotten?

The smoker's world has lost
its hospitality. Nonsmoking
friends send you to the basement
or garage with a tuna can for an ashtray.
Restaurants direct you to concealed smoking
sections or outside. When that becomes unacceptable,
only extraterrestrial smoking will be allowed, hopefully
on planets with enough oxygen to light a cigarette.

Yet, people continue to smoke. Presumably you
are one of them.

People who have never smoked, or who have quit
and become adamantly antismoking, accuse smokers of
being flawed, suicidal risk-takers. Or they denounce
them for lacking the courage to face their addiction.
Trying to cease smoking by getting down on yourself
creates tension, which increases its hold. We do nothing
for ourselves by comparing and condemning ourselves.

If a smoker didn't get something good out of smoking, he wouldn't do it. A person smokes for reasons. This
book will help you discover the role it plays in your life
and to consider alternatives. If you prefer a smoking
cessation program that condemns smoking on principle,
and negatively inspires with aversion techniques, read
no further. This is not for you.

But if you are willing to do an honest self-
evaluation: to see how smoking has contributed positively to your life, and to consider other ways options to
satisfy your needs, this book can help you make a suc-
cessful transition from smoker to nonsmoker.

Change can be exhilarating and joyful, as opposed to something you have to grin and bear through. Still, it is not a quick fix. Looking at oneself honestly requires commitment and courage. And it must be made your own creation, using this outline as a guide. Use what makes sense to you.

In order to make your transition from smoker to nonsmoker, you will consider why and under what circumstances you began to smoke, and why you continued. Be gentle and nonjudgmental. You are not out to prove yourself wrong. You are about to begin a journey with a destination.

By learning about yourself, you can tailor a program uniquely suitable for you. There is no one right way.

YOUR SMOKING HISTORY

Let us return to the room of the double message.

First, make the place more comfortable. Get rid of those awful posters and the "**NO SMOKING**" sign. Reach for your favorite brand. Let the smoke take you back to your first cigarette. Then consider how to proceed.

If you hate essay questions, don't force yourself to write a book. You could use a tape recorder, take notes, or both. If you love to write, however, indulge yourself. The point

is to explore your smoking patterns and personality style.

Do this alone. It is your private time to reflect, not censor or edit. This is you talking to you, not listening to others. Try to be honest, but if you do fudge, simply note it without judging yourself.

HOW YOU STARTED SMOKING

Why did you start smoking? To belong? To rebel? Or both?

Don't criticize, just observe. If memories elicit emotions, let that be all right. You are constructing your personal smoking history, or more accurately, your history that ran concurrent with your smoking.

What were your earliest images of smoking? Hollywood has long associated it with rebellion. Advertisers attempt to influence perception. The Virginia Slims' "You've come a long way, baby" slogan refers to when women who smoked defied social dictates. Marlboro, originally a cigarette for women, portrays macho ruggedness and individualism.

What influenced you when you started smoking? How did that first drag feel? Were you older or younger? Take note of everything.

- Did your parents smoke?
- Did your friends smoke?
- Did you steal cigarettes?
- Did you enjoy the risk of getting caught?
- Did you have a special place to smoke?
- Did you associate smoking with sophistication?

Don't worry if you don't see clear connections between the past and present. Resistance is often part of the process. For the moment, recount your biography, focusing on the cigarette.

Your smoking habit has been your silent companion through it all, yet you are asking yourself to give it up without so much as a passing consideration. Constructing your smoking biography, like eulogizing a deceased friend, gives honor to the relationship and what you shared together.

WHY YOU CONTINUED

What made you persist beyond your first few cigarettes? After the dizzy lightheaded sensation wore off, what were your reasons for continuing? Did it make you feel more sophisticated, adventuresome or independent?

Most of us have experienced a great deal of change. But what hasn't changed?

- Are you still with the same partner?
- Are you in the same house? The same city? The same state?
- How often has your job changed?
- Do you have the same friends you had ten years ago? Twenty years ago?

By investigating your relationship to this paper tube filled with dried, cured plant substance you learn

about yourself. Let your mind float over the scenes. If you enjoyed fishing, hear the rushing stream, smell the pine trees, recall the conversations, and feel the familiar presence of a pack of cigarettes in your shirt pocket.

Memory can be inaccurate. So what! If you wish to exaggerate, go ahead. Make that fish over 20 inches, or minimize: "I wasn't really that obnoxious."

How did circumstance or location affect your smoking?

- Did you smoke more when you changed jobs or work?
- Did your partner smoke?
- Did you change brands with a new partner?
- Did you try to smoke outside when you became a parent?
- What did you wear?
- Were you thin or heavy?
- How did you feel about how you looked?
- Were you under stress?
- Did illness affect your smoking?
- Did finances affect your smoking?
- What was the effect of other's attitudes?
- Did you find it easier to join rather than oppose?

If you haven't yet identified any prominent role the cigarette has played in your life, proceed anyway. I suspect that you will begin to see how something roughly three inches long can be so large.

Don't overlook what might seem trivial. If skeptical, don't give up. Continue. Persisting makes important discoveries inevitable as you prepare to move from smoker to nonsmoker. Don't underestimate the

seductive power of your mind's associations. Photographs may help.

- Were you in the military?
- Were you in school?
- Starting your first job?
- Who was with you when you smoked?
- Who was excluded?
- Did you like to smoke with a special friend?
- Did it give you a place to get away?
- Did it mark you in some way that you liked?

To be a human being is to be a sexual being. What associations do you have with smoking and sex?

- Did a cigarette give you courage to be more aggressive?
- Was it a way of saying, "I am an adult?"
- Did it make you feel more seductive?
- Did it provide distance from intimacy?
- Is sex without the cigarette afterward like cake without icing?

How have these associations changed over the course of your relationships? For example, did a partner's once sexy smoking become annoying? Or was it something that continued to add to your intimacy?

Remember, these lists cannot be all inclusive. Add to them. Write down what comes to mind.

When we experience profound change, for good or bad, our world changes. What were your life transitions? How did they influence your smoking?

- Marriage.
- Death of a parent.
- Falling out with a friend.
- Losing a job.
- Receiving an award.
- Starting your life's work.
- Buying or building a house.
- Climbing a mountain.
- An illness.
- Dyeing your hair.
- A trip to Europe.
- Becoming a parent.
- Losing a pet.
- Starting school.
- Acting in a play.
- Being arrested.

Configure the list to your life. Maybe the mysterious new faces of jazz clubs altered your sense of possibilities. Or, did you feel yourself to be a different person after you got tattooed or divorced? Let your mind go where it will.

Do not forget to include those times, if any, when you quit. What precipitated the decision? What derailed you? Did others try to pressure you to quit?

Your success depends on your own personal readiness and decision. Yet people lean on your guilt buttons.

It is perilous to the wanting-to-quit smoker to hear: "Quit for me" or "Quit for the sake of the children." You may be tempted to quit to shut them up. Don't.

Equally toxic is the glorious idea that you and your partner can quit together, make a pact and help each other out. It's a tempting invitation, and a veritable minefield of detonating possibilities.

What happens to your relationship when he or she says, "Don't worry, I'm having just this one?" Or when you find a floating butt in the toilet? Righteous indignation with your traitorous loved one soon fades into demoralization; it comes down to fight or join. And how will you feel if you are first to break the compact? Forming an alliance to quit smoking is fraught with complications. It is a way to slough off ownership of your own commitment, and can threaten both of your successes.

Have you ever succumbed to the "health panic" motivation? Mysterious aches and pains appear. You read an article and see your arteries shrink while imagining a cancer garden take root in your lungs. Every cigarette brings a sense of impending doom. "I am killing myself," you conclude, and toss your half-empty pack into the trash, then lie awake at night hoping it's not too late. But soon you borrow "just one." With the habit's return comes self-condemnation, "I know I should quit, someday I will," followed by a cavalier, "We

all are going to die of something." The battle rages anew.

My reasons to quit contained the seeds of my undoing. Because I implemented my plan without thinking through how I was to replace what smoking provided, I felt bad, self-insulting and self-punishing. It was a setup for failure.

It's as if a subconscious scribe notes deprivations to demand subsequent payment. Anyone who has ever followed a strict diet with a half gallon of ice cream has faced this baffling principle. Whatever has been taken away must and will be replaced. Have you sabotaged yourself with sudden decisions taken without considering all of your needs? Or, do you plan, plan, and plan, without ever implementing anything? Perhaps a little of both?

MAKING THE CONNECTION

By now you have most likely recorded a significant portion your personal history, its story line, things completed and things left undone. Next, you can set out on making the connections necessary to help you make your decision to stop smoking.

Look through your notes. Note the major events, pivotal points of change, people, accomplishments, and their associations. Starting from your first cigarette, ascertain your needs.

How has the cigarette helped in satisfying your need for:

- Acceptance?
- Individuality?
- Social connections?
- Accomplishment?
- Rest?
- Stimulation?
- Entertainment?

Identify what you liked. Your needs and likes may be compatible: I needed to take the time to walk in the park, and liked the wonderful old trees. Or, in conflict: I needed lots of sleep, but liked working extra hours at night.

How did your smoking fit in with your needs and likes?

When you needed a break and liked to stroll in the park, did you light up a cigarette instead? Or did you sacrifice your need for rest by smoking in order to buy extra work time? Perhaps you were shy, but the job you liked required a need for meetings, which you tolerated behind a wall of smoke.

Our double messages usually indicate confusion between need and like. Do you need to smoke and would like to quit? Or do you like to smoke and need to quit?

Obviously, you have hired the cigarette to do a job. What has it been? How has this habit been of service to you? You are its employer, in a position to evaluate work performance. Has it lived up its promise? Is its current position obsolete? Has it tried to usurp your

position as president of the company? If you decide to dismiss it, what will replace it?

LISTING THE GAINS

Now, list how smoking has benefited you. You may be surprised to find how integral a role this little white cylinder has played in your life. Mine was so long, I began to wonder if I would ever dare let go of such a compelling and useful habit. But this is only one side of the story.

What has done so much for you will, in the light of awareness, lose the benefit of being automatic. It will no longer be the invisible friend who takes care of problems without your notice. Awareness is a double-edged sword: uncomfortable initially, then good in the long run. Habit, when suddenly noticed, loses the very element that makes it habit. Putting as much attention as you can muster on your smoking will further the discomfort—which leads to toppling its status as habit.

Out of the corner of your eye you may have noticed negatives attached to the benefits; ones you've always known, and less obvious ones. For example, if smoking provided distance from people, it also hindered closeness. Or did you take a smoke break instead of going to the gym? Jot down these more elusive negatives when they occur to you. These will be used later on when you compile your grounds for dismissal.

The gain list can be a guide to create new ways to meet these needs. But it also makes you conscious of what has become habit, so automatic, so part of your experience, that you rarely give it an objective glance. Even the familiar—typing, breathing, and walking—can sound and feel weird under the light of conscious awareness.

GETTING CURRENT

Now you will list the present day benefits. Pick three days, different days, such as a routine workday, a rest day (hopefully you have one of those), and a chore day. If all your days are alike, use three different routines to observe how your smoking varies according to your activities.

THE THREE DAY DIARY

Journal the details of when and where you smoke, how long between cigarettes, and your thoughts as you smoke. Don't evaluate or judge, simply observe. Wear the white lab coat of the objective scientist.

Keep in mind this exercise's long-lasting benefit. Awareness can set you free.

For the moment, be the scrupulous scribe, and don't miss a scrap of trivia. You will have plenty of time to ponder implications later.

Do you smoke:

- With particular people?
- Different brands?
- In the parking lot?
- In the basement?
- In the bathroom?

- While driving?
- After sex?
- With a drink?
- After dinner?
- With coffee?
- In a bar?
- At your desk?
- In bed?

My first reaction to my entry was its boringness. I didn't want to see how mundane a role the cigarette played in my life. Yet on closer examination, I saw how it met many of my needs. I took out two pieces of paper, on one I wrote Benefits, on the other Negatives.

When I began I associated smoking with image, sophistication, and access to certain people. But these benefits were no longer forthcoming. I no longer felt attractive when smoking. My habit was a bone of contention with my partner, and even though my daughter and I shared smoking together, I felt guilty for

encouraging her habit by way of example. Although it was relaxing and rewarding, it caused tension, and did nothing for my self-esteem.

Earlier you were asked to identify how smoking contributed positively to your life. Now, what about cigarettes don't you like? Continue to be objective. Do you:

- Smoke first thing in the morning or right before bed?
- Cough?
- Rationalize your smoking?
- Fill jars with butts and ash?
- Occasionally fall asleep with a lit cigarette?
- Become angry when someone complains about your smoke?

Feel free to personalize this list.

Comparing my current smoking status to my smoking history helped me realize: 1) Certain fundamental needs were still being met by smoking, and 2) I was paying a high price to get those needs met.

Imagine doing a job review with the cigarette as your employee. How well is it doing? Are aspects of its job obsolete? What, if anything, in its job description is indispensable? If smoking at one time helped you rebel, and you now see such a statement to the world irrelevant, you may be able to dispense with that one. But if, for example, smoking helped your creativity, you will need to devise another way to do this or you will find yourself frustrated.

FILLING IN THE HOLES

You may be tempted to skip over your reasons to smoke in favor of the obvious reasons to quit. After all, isn't

that the objective? Dwelling on the positives may seem counterintuitive.

Yet *Filling in the Holes* is not about finding a substitute for smoking. It is about recognizing your individual needs and creating balance in your life without tobacco. Then, when life challenges you (as it surely will) and you are tempted (as you will be), you will be able to manage the emotional longing for the comfort of a cigarette without succumbing to your familiar pattern.

Without this old friend, how do you think you will you feel? Lonely? Agitated? Bored? Afraid? Restless? What, exactly, would be missing without your cigarette? What are the holes?

Your diary will help. Be specific. For example, when I fumbled for a cigarette in the middle of the night, I reached for an old reliable pal. Without it, would I lie awake, ill at ease? I considered my relationships, thought of my spiritual life, and questioned if I could I allow myself to accept loneliness as part of life.

Nature abhors a vacuum, and so do our psyches. If you smoked to combat boredom, you won't be satisfied with an uninteresting smokeless life. You want to make sure your holes will not be filled with undesirables which could drive you back to your habit. If your work breaks were smoke breaks, you may find yourself cranky and just plain miserable. You needed that time away, filling it with more work will not serve you.

What could fill the gap? A book? Television? Meditation? Few smokers are aware of tobacco's spiritual and ancient heritage.

Every culture has used plants to change consciousness. Imagine some distant ancestor inhaling burning cannabis and saying, "Hey man, that's good sh_." Life for Homo erectus was never the same. The ancient Egyptians drank beer after a hard day of pyramid building. Indigenous South Americans chewed coca. Converted into fine white powder, this same plant has become a major threat to vast segments of our population.

Tobacco, a large leafed member of the nightshade family with white or pink flowers, possesses mind-altering chemicals. It obviously changes consciousness. It may be less apparent how it creates a sacred space. Yet every time you smoke to gain perspective, to get a little distance, to take a time out, you are, to some degree, converting the ordinary into the holy. If you smoke to facilitate thinking or creativity, you are casting out matter in search of inspiration. Smoke is the messenger.

Part earth, part air, smoke is considered by many cultures to be a messenger between spirit and matter. Native Americans use it in ritual to carry prayers to the Great Spirit. Smoke from incense purifies and sanctifies temples and churches throughout the world. The word "perfume" comes from the French *parfume*, which means through smoke: used not only for its aromatic properties but as a means to connect to God and each other.

With ever increasing demands on our time, with more and more pressure to perform and to be

productive, comes its opposite: the inner demand for peace, stillness, nonproductivity, the need to just be. It is not aberration to want a holy place. Even if we do not subscribe to traditional religion, we still want to experience reverence and gratefulness. Smoking can be viewed as a prayer. It provides time to reflect and shift focus. If to any degree, smoking has done that for you, you will not be able to ignore its absence. It can hatch an unwanted hole in your life. Some people meditate to fill it, others walk in nature. You will need to put in place whatever replenishes you.

Take time to review your typical and quirky needs. Do you absolutely need to begin your day with a dose of the outdoors, regardless of the weather? Smokers, especially if indoor smoking was taboo, may depend on that ten-minute exposure to the elements—time to watch squirrels, ocean waves, icicles melt, or children walk to school. Don't give these up just because you don't have a cigarette as an excuse. If you enjoy conversation and banter with smoking friends, continue. You want to gain more than you lose as you make the transition from smoker to nonsmoker.

It is not necessary to follow these steps in strict sequence. You will probably zigzag around a bit. I began with positive reasons to smoke to avoid the trap of negative-based motivations.

GROUNDS FOR DISMISSAL

Out of the negative data emerged what I call *Grounds for Dismissal*, which come from your courageous self-examination and evaluation, not pressure from magazine articles or people's disapproval. Take the

time you need. Be the objective scientist, wear your white lab coat. Collect negative data, but don't include yourself in the data. You are not a bad person for smoking. Let the habit be the negative, not you.

This is not easy. For years you have heard family, friends, doctors, and strangers criticize, threaten and plead. But the most dangerous voice can be your own. Be nice to yourself while collecting these negatives. If one of your *Grounds for Dismissal* is that smoking stinks, keep in mind you did not hire the cigarette in order to stink. The culprit is the cigarette; you may smell perfectly fine on your own, but tobacco and its additives change your odor. Not a nice thing to face. Nevertheless, you must be kind to yourself. You are evaluating the cigarette's job performance and it has failed you. The negative is clear: smoking stinks. But the positive is also clear: if you were no longer a smok-

er, you wouldn't stink, at least not from tobacco. Out of your negative list comes your positives.

You are the boss. The cigarette, your employee, has overstepped his job, went beyond the original terms of employment, and decided to be chairman of the board. He somehow took over, as addictive substances eventually will.

But you are regaining charge. How has smoking failed you?

Your *Grounds for Dismissal* need to be in align-ment with your unique way of seeing things. You could write it out in list form, or do a presentation as though you were the chairman submitting it to board members. You likely will notice inner disagreements. For exam-ple, you may not like how smoking congests your throat, yet an inner board member likes your husky voice. The habit of smoking is deeply rooted in all your parts, and they are not always in agreement. It is not necessarily a logical thing. Expect disputes.

THE INNER JUDGE

An inner judge, without grace or humor, criticizes and castigates. When that part accuses you of being worthless and beyond hope, another part replies: "I'll show you." This is the "child" of your "inner parent," who rebels against all of your best intentions in trying to protect your ego. People who try to motivate themselves by focusing on the negatives often don't acknowledge the power of this inner child.

The inner judge loves the word "should," especial-ly in combination with negative descriptions. Thinking, "I should stop smoking because it is a disgusting habit," can feel like, "I am a disgusting". The thought, "Smoking is going to kill me," can feel like "I am irresponsible, incapable of taking care of myself." Such thinking tears you to shreds. Is this the condition you want to be in when you decide to stop smoking? If you weaken your-self with continual reminders of what a terrible person you are for smoking, how do you expect to have the strength

to commit to stop? Be careful not to pulverize yourself when listing your *Grounds for Dismissal.*

The subconscious ignores the word "not". If you repeat to yourself, "I am not sick," it hears "I am sick." The "not" slithers by your awareness like a slippery eel. Rather, to use affirmation effectively, say "I am healthy." Instead of writing, "Smoking wrinkles me up like a California Raisin," recognize you value your appearance, and regard quitting as a chance to mani-fest this value by scheduling facials, using good moisturizers, or possibly getting a face lift. Turn the negatives into positives. Each time we do something that supports a positive belief we get closer to the exit of the "Nightmare Room," the place of the double message.

COLLECTING THE POSITIVES

The mind follows pleasure. Even negative thinking must offer some pleasure for the mind to entertain it. *Collecting Positives* considers what you will gain by becoming a nonsmoker. It constructs a path you will want to travel.

Our minds can be maddeningly complex; fickle and busy, like a monkey hopping from branch to branch, swinging one moment and stopping to scratch an itch the next. We long to be a unified whole, yet are more often an unruly committee. What the mind finds perfectly reasonable may be rejected by the emotions. What satisfies the body may crumple the spirit. Invari-ably, whenever we begin to make a resolve, a part of ourselves comes up with reasons why it won't work. Our inner committees go after simplicity with the ven-geance of a band of starving hyenas.

The "health nut" part not only wants to stop smok-ing, but thinks you should go on a cleansing fast. The

"hedonist" rationalizes a relaxing smoke after dinner. The "pleaser" wants to placate your nagging mate, while the "rebel teenager" wants to blow smoke in everybody's face.

We associate confusion with weakness, have the mistaken notion that willpower should silence those conflicting elements, and envy the person who just quits—without fanfare, hypnosis, special techniques, books, patches, or expensive seminars. Yet the heart's antagonism to the mind's dictates supports addiction.

Denying parts of ourselves only infuriates the dragon and perpetuates the inner war. Maybe we need to admit we aren't going to find a quick fix. But a compassionate understanding of self is a place to begin. From there we can make the necessary journey to commitment. We are many-faceted, and success is only possible through the coordinated effort of both mind and heart, body and the spirit.

A positive sense of self, however, is not the same as the swaggering self that thinks: "I can stop anytime I want." Arrogance, a false sense of power, is an enemy. It is necessary to call forth the small inner voice that is able to say in humility, "I am willing."

Collecting Positives considers your mental, emotional, physical and spiritual needs. You will not be willing to relinquish a satisfying habit unless you convince yourself you will be happier without it. It is more than seeing nonsmoking as merely a good idea, it is starting to imagine yourself as a nonsmoker.

How will it look to actually be a nonsmoker? Your positive imagination can stimulate your will, pulling it along until you are ready to consider letting go of your smoking habit. See it on your screen of possibilities— not a mental dictate to rebel against, nor a rash decision motivated by middle-of-the-night panic—but a resolve constructed from a serious and comprehensive look at what you want for yourself.

Many people underestimate the hold the habit has on them. But you know letting go is not an easy task. In order to be ready to quit, you need make a self-agreement that considers your many agendas. Your habit, especially if you have smoked for a long time, has developed a complicated root system. If you have ever had a garden overtaken by mint, the gopher of the plant kingdom, with its ferocious tap roots, you know what kind of perseverance it can take to get rid of this hearty herb. If you don't get all the roots you will have mint until the day you die. It would be nice if our habits were like succulents with shallow roots you can move about your garden like chess pawns. But we are dealing with "mint," and it ain't easy. Although the exercises offered thus far are helpful, they are not strong enough, in and of themselves, to take you the full route.

MAKING A COMMITMENT

The destination is the place where we make a promise. *Collecting Positives* paves the path. But we will never reach it if we wait for perfection, for all conflicts to be settled and all holes filled. On the other hand, hurrying

with insufficient understanding can lead to a rash promise we don't quite mean.

THE KEY TO YOUR SUCCESS

We rarely associate *commitment* to the everyday, small things in life. Rather, we reserve "commitment" to where it really counts.

Once a friend asked if I could promise not to eat a bagel for a week. I said, "Sure."

A week later he asked if I had kept my commitment. I had, but was not very impressed—I'd eaten all sorts of other foods I thought bad for me. But, no, I hadn't eaten a bagel. Big deal.

Nonetheless, I kept my promise. He congratulated me and claimed I now understood *commitment*. I disagreed because I doubted I would have kept it if it were known only to myself. He replied that it didn't matter if the commitment were to him, to myself, or to God—the power was in keeping one's word.

For *commitment* to work, we need to look at it differently. The problem with personal ethics is that we are in charge, we make the rules, we execute them. That's a lot of responsibility. If we fail to follow our own standards, we have no one else to blame. We are quick to do the right thing for someone else; we are much less willing to do the right thing for ourselves.

In our complex, pluralistic society, integrity requires personal guidelines. The Native American expression "Walk your talk" was easier to do in a tribal community. Binding agreements that bind are less the norm. Although holding fast to a vow that no longer serves anyone is foolish, there is a place for unconditional promises. The concept of commitment, as it is used here, is never a "maybe" or "we shall see," but a definite

"for sure." Therefore, the commitment must be in align·
ment with a spiritual principle, it must be made with
integrity. To make a commitment is to "walk your talk."
Once a commitment is drafted and underway, there is
no longer room for fudging.

We all belong to societies and organizations that
adhere to certain principles and laws. Yet without per·
sonal ethics we would be mindless robots. We do have
our own laws. The question is, do we follow them?

MAKE THE COMMITMENT CLEAR

You want to understand your commitment fully, to elim·
inate any room to backslide when your "good idea" no
longer looks so good. Write down your draft. Let the
words settle on the page. Examine them for clarity and
specificity.

A commitment is always to some action, not a
quality. For example, a commitment "to be nicer to my
mother·in·law" is vague. A more specific commitment
would look like: "I promise to send my mother-in-law a
positive note each week. As a trial, I will do this for a
month beginning _____ and ending _____ ."

Whether the note is one sentence or three pages
doesn't matter. How you felt while writing it—
relief, anger, or fear—also doesn't
matter. You cannot legislate feel·
ings. You commit to action. A
promise to be a happy nonsmok·
er is unreasonable. How do you
evaluate success? How happy is
happy? Keep your commitments
simple, and keep them possible.
Don't include feelings. Some days might
be miserable: this must not affect your

resolve. Feelings could change as a consequence of action, but committing to a feeling leads to a confusing mire.

Only you can be responsible for your commitment. It is simpler to restrict your commitments to those of your own actions, depending on others incurs risks that eclipse any possible support.

PLACE THE COMMITMENT IN TIME

In addition to making your commitment concrete and specific, you need to place your vow in time (not *Time* the magazine). A promise without date or duration is like whistling in a gale. Be aware of the lurking sabo-teur within who loves to find loopholes.

"Let's see, did I say I would stop smoking for a year, a month, or until it gets too hard?" That line of thinking, sooner or later, can crack any resolve.

The Alcoholics Anonymous "One day at a time" keeps a person in the moment, out of the scary future with its multitude possibilities of failure—and keeps at bay the frightening, overwhelming concept of forever. Yet the internal saboteur can whisper all manner of rationale: "Just this one. You can pay it back, tomorrow." When this crazy thinking threatens to take over, a support system—friend, sponsor, meeting—can help correct the error. You cannot afford to let this kind of thinking take root, and it could if you do not place your smoking commitment in time.

You need an airtight system, which may feel terrible. The part that says, "I'll never say never," is appalled. But what is the alternative? If you give yourself the possibility of a cigarette, chances are one day down the road you will take this possibility and make it a reality.

Ralph Waldo Emerson wrote: "Our faith comes in moments; our vice is habitual. Yet there is a depth in those brief moments which constrains us to ascribe more reality to them than to all other experiences."

Frame your commitment in such a way to not alarm your internal rebel. If you think of yourself as quitting smoking, you enhance the sense of loss. Thinking of it as a gift, rather than a deprivation, can make it forever.

Roll this idea around a bit in your mind: On a given day I will say: "As of _____, I am a nonsmoker."

You. Yes, you, can choose a new identity. This may seem farfetched or impossible, but please read on.

TRANSCENDING YOUR ORDINARY SELF

Making your commitment to someone or something that transcends your ordinary self can guarantee conversion to nonsmoker because you evoke the presence of "another."

Although this seems to contradict making the process personal and not involving others, promising the little self who constantly looks for ways to rebel is fruitless. Our wobbly vows (ones we secretly know we won't keep) are made to this small self. Her specialty is letting us down, and we end up feeling powerless. It is this recognition of powerlessness that Alcoholics Anonymous calls the first step to recovery. The next is giving yourself over to a "higher power."

What you call that power is entirely up to you. Most of us are willing to concede that there exists a being, ideal, or energy source outside our myopic perceptions. How you perceive this presence depends on your beliefs. You might feel it to be God, a guardian angel, or, in more secular terms, a "big self" that is

transcendent of the smaller ego. This presence enables access to a wisdom ordinarily out of our reach.

A commitment made in alignment with an unlimited supply of power, combined with your bit of willingness, meets up with this unending source. You may think this is much ado about nothing, but again consider what you are up against. Smoking is no small habit. A fly swatter will not serve you well in the company of a lion.

Choose your source of help accordingly. Whatever systems you choose, whatever deities or principles you select to assist you, be aware that you are submitting yourself to something beyond your ordinary capabilities.

Every triumph, and every goal achieved, increases confidence, which can cause a remarkable shift in consciousness. The world suddenly looks brighter, cleaner, and more hopeful.

CEREMONIAL BEGINNING

Ceremony evokes power. It facilitates movement. All cultures and religions mark changes of the mind, heart, and spirit with ceremony. Whether it's raising the right hand in making an oath, or immersion in baptismal water, the body feels the earnestness of ritual. A touch or hug makes saying "I love you" more real. Ritual fires the necessary neurons to make a memory dent, an inroad to the place where success lies.

Your ceremony needs to be tangible. Trying to change behavior with thought alone, especially with a

history of broken resolutions, can be muddling. Physi-
cality alerts your brain: something different is about to
occur, you mean business. Your personal ethics will
have more clout when the urge of habit threatens to
melt your resolve like an ice cube on a hot summer day.
Rather than thinking "Forget it, that's just the way I
am," ceremony proclaims: "What I say, I will do. What I
was, I am no longer."

Whether you simply tap your foot, or light a hun-
dred candles, it is a spiritual act. You gaze into the
mirror, see yourself perform, wake up, and become more
conscious.

Your resolve should be clear and concrete, placed
in time, and made in the presence of another: whether
God, your angel or higher self. Ceremony invokes this
presence. It connects your intention—to stop doing
something that makes you uncomfortable—to the pow-

er that has the strength to
carry it out. The ceremo-
ny's physical expression
alerts your mind, keeping
you focused as you summon
your personal source of
energy. Even if you don't
use bells and incense, it
should have personal mean-
ing. It can be as simple as a
finger snap, which could be
your "call to action," or a
foot tap to remind you of
your connection to the
earth.

PRACTICE PUTTING COMMITMENT INTO ACTION

You can practice the process with a behavior or habit less challenging than smoking. It will help you see *commitment* as a workable tool, not merely an abstract concept.

Identify where you collapse into your usual forms of avoidance and rationalization, then begin with simple commitments. Designate specific, and short, time parameters—15 minutes, a half hour, or half a day. If you must go longer, try to make it less than a week. The point is to experience the power of commitment through repeated successes, not to weed out every behavior you don't like.

For example, suppose you hate hospitals, but have promised to visit a sick friend. On the way out you catch sight of a movie you rented, and think to watch only a few minutes. Soon you can't tear yourself away, which means missing visiting hours. You don't feel good about your decision, but rationalize, "Oh well, there's always tomorrow." Although a nagging voice inside keeps you from fully enjoying the movie, you stay on the couch. Then you remember your commitment, decide to watch the movie after the visit, and enact your ritual: You do a double finger snap, cross your eyes, and hit the off button.

You stopped an uncomfortable behavior that clashed with a personal ethic. One that in the past you felt compelled to continue.

DRAFTING THE COMMITMENT

Once made and sealed by ceremony, it should be nonnegotiable. Consider carefully the content of your promise. If you fear that what seems to be a good idea might look less attractive in the future, negotiate a clause.

Writing law is difficult. Interpretation is even harder. Just look at our judicial system. We don't want to hire a lawyer to deal with ourselves, but we do want to watch for loopholes to avoid disputes with those shifty, dishonest parts inside who will do anything to "break the law."

Pay attention to your words. Does after dinner include the middle of the night? Do holidays include Save the Lemming Week? These interpretations defy the spirit of your resolve, which was to replace the addictive behavior with a nonaddictive one. Do not leave proposed self-legislation open to interpretations by that part who cares not a tinker's damn about the spirit of yours or anyone else's law.

It is humbling to realize the inner self-saboteur can have such a grip. It has been working against our behalf for a long time, and has many clever ways to undo our best efforts. You must be smarter than it when drafting your commitment. This takes practice.

The correction and punishment paradigm can make it difficult to see commitment as a gift to yourself. Feeling punished and deprived sets the stage for future rebellion. *Commitment* is not a punitive tool, designed to make you good but miserable. It adds something pleasurable.

STATE OF GRACE

The *State of Grace* is the light, the city of gold, the beautiful princess, the prince charming: the reward for finally understanding that you do not have to do it all by yourself. It comes from giving an addictive behavior over to the process. *State of Grace* is the condition of a person thus influenced.

Commitment elicits this power. You solicit help from an infallible source, to strengthen your resolve, while no longer weakened by the addiction. When up against a destructive habit we tend to believe we deserve punishment; the most efficient way to met out that punishment is to continue the harmful habit. Grace forgives, springing this trap of self-defeating behavior.

A definition of grace is "divine influence acting in man to make him pure and morally strong." Addiction, regardless of its type—from chocolate to cocaine—promises relief from discomfort. Awareness blows our covers, unravels our rationalizations. Actions out of alignment with our higher good, once done to avoid discomfort, start to cause discomfort when we are willing to commit to change. We have put ourselves in a place where grace can happen.

Smoking has brought you benefits, and problems. Understanding the *State of Grace* keeps you from running in a circle, chasing and being chased by the double message. You may come to see your addiction as a gift: a lesson on the importance of transcending old definitions of self. In contrast to the agitation you felt, as you connect your commitment to a power source via ritual, you will experience relief and freedom.

When you first looked at your addiction squarely, with reality glasses on, you stirred the pot; all sorts of not-so-nice critters floated to the top. Some flew in your face. Others may have taken you by surprise with covert actions. But they all cursed you.

Sealing your commitment ceremony surrenders your habit to an energy that transcends your ordinary self. The hard battle is the surrender.

Imagine running in a deluge, shivering with cold and fear of lightning, while water pours through your hair and down your limbs. Finally, you come upon a hospitable house. Inside, you sit beside a warm fireplace, with dry clothes and a hot drink. Outside, the storm continues, but it is not the same reality for you anymore. This is the *State of Grace.*

Don't worry if this seems too good to be true. Practice short-duration commitments using an uncomplicated ritual-reminder. Begin to experience positive results. What you can do in five minutes, you can do in a week, in a month, in a year, in a lifetime. But start small. Commit only to things that are relatively painless. Set your intention, offer it to the energy source of your choice, and then experience the feeling of protection and freedom that comes from living more deliberately and with greater connection. Don't worry about those things you don't like about yourself, but are not yet willing to change.

Notice how you feel before, on the edgy discomfort of being out of harmony, and contrast it to how you feel once you have performed your ceremony and put your commitment into place. Grace is also gratitude.

Will this "grace" stuff really work? It will if you believe it will. You always have a choice. You can believe in the process or not.

Since it is of greater benefit to believe in it and no harm will come to you if you do, you may

as well tell your skeptical self to take a hike while prac-
ticing until you gain a measure of confidence.

SOME ADDITIONAL CONSIDERATIONS

What if it fails?

If you did not make a provision for the unexpect-
ed, you learn.

In the case of unforeseen circumstances, remember the spirit versus the letter of the law.

What if you simply forget? You may need to pay
more attention: to practice focus and awareness.

What if you collapse into the sudden impulse of
the moment? Does that prove that this process is a
waste of time? Not at all. Unless you decide to give up,
as proof that here is one more thing that won't work for
you, you can simply dust yourself off and begin anew.

Commitment teaches honesty, reliability, trust-
worthiness. Virtues that serve well in any life endeavor.

APPOINTMENT WITH YOURSELF

Timing is important. You want to be sure that you have
completed your smoking career. Be kind
to yourself. If you don't know how you
will get through a difficult time at work
without smoking, perhaps you should
wait. You want to give yourself as much
advantage as possible. If adding another month to
your smoking will help insure success, then do it.

Return to the room of the double message. Take
down those awful posters. Sit back, light up, and
consider a good time to stop. Look at your calendar.
Give this the consideration it deserves. Would it be best
before, on, or after a vacation? A time when you know
you will be alone? When you have selected a date, mark

your calendar. You have made an appointment with yourself.

MORE PREPARATION

Continue to practice commitment up until your last smoking day. Take notice of new observations and insights. Watch your thoughts and emotions. Are you confident or fearful? Try to address the negatives; when you can, substitute them with positives. If you fear gaining weight, consider, rather, that food will taste better, and you don't have to be a glutton. Take the time to understand any doubt you may feel. If you have thoughts like, "How will I party without a cigarette?" or "I will miss that smoke before bed when I think about the day," don't try to sweep them under the rug. They are real. Work through these scenarios and find a positive gift for yourself. It doesn't have to be tangible, perhaps simply the good feeling that comes from attending a party as a nonsmoker.

Compare the pluses to the minuses. You may find yourself looking forward to stopping—no more labored breathing going up the stairs, no more hassle of keeping up with smoking supplies. Maybe you can hardly wait.

You may want to do some research on the needs of your body. Patches, gum, or herbal formulas may assist with the physical discomfort of nicotine withdrawal. Your doctor, pharmacist, and health food store can be valuable resources. If you are not a water drinker, think about becoming one. Water is excellent for flushing out toxins. Eat your fruits, vegetables, whole grains, and low-fat protein. But for heaven's sake, don't be a puritan. With your taste buds coming alive, enjoy palatable pleasures, but do try to enjoy with some measure of moderation.

If your psyche can't take too much health at once, give yourself something wicked from time to time. A double chocolate anything is recommended, occasionally. Some contend that coffee and alcohol should be avoided because of their association with smoking. I found, however, a cup of java helpful.

I associated coffee, like cigarettes, with being an adult, and was not, in my newly acquired state of non-smoking, going to head for the milk and graham crackers. You will have to make these decisions for yourself. But nothing—what you eat or drink, whether you visit the library or the smokiest bar in town—should loosen your resolve. Still, it is wise to make yourself as comfortable as possible. If coffee and alcohol send you into fits, by all means avoid them.

Although small-time addictions can help get you through that edgy period, we do not want to substitute one addiction for another. Please be careful.

A morning coffee or dinner wine are probably not symptoms of addiction. To become a gum-aholic might not do much for your image, and if you chew the sugared kind, for your teeth, either. But it doesn't qualify as a particularly harmful addiction. I must admit that for a time I became utterly dependent on chewing gum.

Deep breathing can help. Most of us don't breathe very well, taking short shallow breaths and forgetting entirely about our belly. Since smoking cigarettes is, let's face it, a breathing exercise, we want to make sure we continue. Now is the time to learn to get your hit

from oxygen, not tobacco. You will be amazed to discover the high it provides.

Exercise ensures good breathing. That annoying shortness of breath will lesson, and stamina will improve. Our lungs have a wondrous ability to recover from the worst abuse. While you exercise, imagine your former grungy lungs turning pink as a baby's bottom.

DESIGNING YOUR QUITTING SMOKING CEREMONY

You need not concern yourself with either brevity or visibility. There are no rules, no judges, and no grades. You can go all out with pomp and circumstance, or you can make it simple and unadorned. Give yourself as much privacy and time as you need. It might be a lengthy decree read aloud with candles ablaze; or a short oath, written, signed, dated, and placed in a special envelope. A personal ceremony gives you permission to be the authority, to modify the conventional to suit your needs. Or to bypass convention altogether, and do your own thing.

But be clear to maximize your receptivity to the help you are soliciting.

Most rituals make use of symbol. Do you have something that symbolizes your personal God, guardian angel or spiritual helper? Look for objects that have personal power for you: a painting, a gold cross, the ring worn by your grandfather, a certain book, a feather, or perhaps a small statue of a saint.

Consider basic ceremonial elements: the four directions (north, south, east, west); the fundamental tools of nature (fire, air, earth, water); the sun, moon and stars; colors, sounds, smells, and so on. You could consider familiar, contemporary rituals such as Catholic Mass, graduation, or the launching of a ship. Or, you

could study an ancient ritualistic practice—not to earn a degree in anthropology—but to expose yourself to ceremonial elements common to the human experience. What is important is that you construct, at least this one time, a meaningful and personal ceremony to mark your transition from smoker to nonsmoker.

One man wrote a divorce decree separating himself from smoking. A woman slipped out of an old smoky dress and put on a new white robe. A longtime smoker laid out three cigarettes; designating the past, the present, and letting go. He smoked each, and then buried the butts under a tree. A young woman made a collage out of her last pack, glued the last butt to her design, hung it on the wall, and never smoked again. Another heavy smoker dumped his last four butts into the river.

Whatever you choose, it marks your decision. It empowers you to be fully engaged and present. You are honoring yourself.

APPENDIX

Excerpts from:

Cynthia's Journal

In my Colorado Rockies days we smoked boldly, discussing philosophy at local restaurants, filling the atmosphere with ideas and the ashtray with stubs. I remember a friend saying, while watching cigarette smoke curl, "You know, you can learn a lot about yourself through a cigarette." I winced. I had just started back up after having quit for over a year.

I resumed by smoking butts. It allowed me to kid myself into thinking I wasn't really smoking. Then I smoked three real cigarettes in a row before burying the rest in my garden, hoping the symbolic act would put my habit into its final resting place. I was fooling myself, by that evening I wanted more. But instead of buying, I dug up that pack. It felt vaguely familiar. Since childhood I've a penchant for being either very good or very bad. When I finally did successfully quit, I used this tendency to my advantage.

In college I was distressed by my wholesome appearance. I wanted to be sophisticated, sexy, poetic. This image required my disassociation with those who didn't smoke, drink, or break rules.

I felt smarter, smoking made me feel more at home with philosophical esoterica. I inhaled obscurities with every inhalation. My friend helped me tick off the hours during all night study session. I measured my Herculean efforts by the amount of cigarette butts in the ashtray. And I smoked so I wouldn't eat. Some women in the dormitory who missed their boyfriends back home ate ice cream to ease their suffering. Not me. I grabbed a cigarette and contemplated Kieregaard and Camus.

I once quit in a fit of punishing self-dislike, hoping the extra sting would finally get this monkey off of my back. Normally I filled long hours on the road with smoking, to stay awake and to stay calm in traffic. I tore down the highway without my crutch , clutching the wheel, each mile a celebration of deprivation. Although I arrived at my destination tattered and worn, a nonsmoking person, my resolve was short lived. Odd behaviors began to surface. I took to lighting things, candles, incense, and finally cigars. It wasn't long until I resumed my smoking with renewed gusto.

When I returned home from college, I lit up with dad, who smoked unfiltered Kools. We spent evenings on the porch in the cool California air. At last, my father and I had a commonalty. I was grown up.

POSITIVES:
- ✓ A friend in the middle of the night.
- ✓ Something to relax me so I could get back to sleep.
- ✓ Time to myself--just sitting on the porch.
- ✓ Work break to gain new perspective.
- ✓ A way to get through my work schedule.
- ✓ A reward.
- ✓ Bonding time with my daughter. Something we could do together.
- ✓ Stress release for emotional upsets.
- ✓ Combat boredom.
- ✓ Something to look forward to.
- ✓ The pleasant completion of a meal.

NEGATIVES:
- ✓ The bother of having to keep track of my cigarettes
- ✓ Taking time out in the morning to buy more.
- ✓ Distraction from my schedule, taking time out to supply my habit.
- ✓ Produced guilt. My fault that my daughter smokes.
- ✓ My fault if I get a dreaded disease.
- ✓ Promoted self-distrust. Promising myself I wouldn't have a cigarette and then going back on my word.
- ✓ Masked my emotions. I smoked to keep back unpleasant feelings.
- ✓ Made me feel bad about myself. I felt unclean and irresponsible to my health.
- ✓ Caused me to be judgmental towards myself and others who smoked.

MONDAY

I woke at 3:00 a.m. and couldn't get back to sleep. I couldn't find my pack. Finally, I found a broken cigarette at the bottom of my purse, which I taped. Pretty stupid, but I was desperate. I didn't wake up until 9:00, which made me mad. I felt behind and hadn't even started my day. I made coffee, but stopped the coffee maker, might as well have coffee out since I had to buy cigarettes anyway. Then I remembered my favorite coffee shop just turned "smoke free."

Whatever happened to the days when a person could drink coffee and smoke in public? I decided to buy cigarettes and return home after all. I bought a carton, returned home, restarted the coffee, and poured myself a cup, and sat on the back porch. I really ought to stop smoking inside. Glad it was warm, I hate smoking outside when it's cold. How can you relax when you are freezing to death? The sun was nice and warm and my cigarette tasted good. These are the times when I really enjoy smoking. I put my cigarette out and dropped it into a special can by the door. I started working at my desk and did OK for awhile, but then hit a block, lit up a cigarette, and blew smoke out the window. That seemed to get my flow going, so I reached for another cigarette and didn't bother to direct my smoke outside. I reasoned that it's my house and if I want to smoke in it, so what. I made toast, drank coffee, and smoked another, four cigarettes in less than two hours. I thought of how I was going to die of something awful with no one to blame but myself, and how my daughter probably wouldn't be smoking if not for me. My fault. Guilt made me think of Paul, who nags me to quit.

Around 3:00 I took a break, had a sandwich, then another cigarette I felt I deserved. My mind cleared. I had already smoked over a half a pack, and was thinking to smoke less tomorrow. By 6:00 I felt a little out of sorts and called it quits. I cleaned out my car and emptied out the full ashtray.

My daughter dropped by and we went out to dinner. At least we agreed about the smoking section. We split a piece of chocolate cheese cake and ordered coffee. The cigarette after that was really the best. I decided not to smoke anymore until just before bed, but when I got home I forgot my resolve and had two more while talking to Paul on the telephone.

Share the Message

Are you interested in:

☐ Bulk copies of *Smoke and Mirrors* for your organization?

☐ Special Editons with your organization or company imprint?

☐ Workshops or training for workshop facilitators based on the principles of this book?

Email Richie@rocketmail.com or mail this form.

Name_____

Street_____

Apt. # _____

City _____State _____ Zip _____

Telephone (_____)_____

Comments:

Cynthia Thorson writes novels, short stories, and practices massage therapy, in Grand Rapids, Michigan.

Richard Levine has facilitated psycho-educational groups since 1984. He also writes screenplays and books, in Jacksonville, Florida.

Printed in the United States
36608LVS00005B/343-441